## 101 THINGS TO DO WITH

# HORRENDOUS HANGOVERS

*Disclaimer:* This book is intended for adults only.
Please enjoy alcohol responsibly.

First published in 2024 by Allsorted Ltd, WD19 4BG U.K.

The facts and statistics in this book are correct up to the end of 2022. Data comes from publicly available sources and is presented as correct as far as our knowledge allows. Any views or opinions represented in this book are personal and belong solely to the book author and are not intended to malign any religious community, ethnic group, club, organization, company or individual.

No part of this work may be reproduced in any form or by any means, electronic or mechanical, including photocopying, recording or by any information storage and retrieval system, without the prior written permission of the publisher.

© 2024 Saturday Publishing Ltd © 2024 Allsorted Ltd
All Rights Reserved.

ISBN 9781915902733

Saturday Publishing Ltd have asserted their rights under the Copyright, Designs and Patents Act, 1988, to be identified as the authors of this work.

Printed in Lithuania.

# *101 THINGS* TO SOOTHE ...
# HORRENDOUS HANGOVERS

ALLSORTED.
WD19 4BG U.K.

# INTRODUCTION

We've all been there – the morning after a night of revelry, when the world seems a little too bright and every sound feels like a drumbeat in your head. **101 Things to Soothe Horrendous Hangovers** is here to rescue you from the depths of your post-party despair. This light-hearted guide is filled with fun activities to distract you and help you navigate the rough seas of a hangover. It's a gentle reminder that even the worst mornings can be turned around with a bit of humour and the right distractions

# 1.

# APPRECIATE THE ANTIQUITY OF ALCOHOL

**Did you know that one of the oldest-known recipes in the world is for beer?**

Written more than 4,000 years ago, it was found on a Sumerian clay tablet in what is now Iraq

# 2.

## HEADACHE HYDROTHERAPY

Time how fast you can drink a big glass of water and see if you can beat the Guinness World Record holder, Tim Cocker, who drank half a litre of water in 1.75 seconds on 9 December 2014. Just don't do this challenge again and again in quick succession – water intoxication is an actual thing, you know

# LEARN HOW TO SAY "HANGOVER" IN DIFFERENT LANGUAGES

Maybe expressing your predicament in a foreign tongue will make it more glamorous and less shameful. Maybe not. Here are three exotic idioms for starters:

1. **French:** *La gueule de bois* ("the wooden mouth")
2. **German:** *Der Kater* ("the tomcat")
3. **Spanish:** *la resaca* ("the backwash")

# 4.

# HANGOVER APPRECIATION DAY

Instead of wallowing in self-pity, take a moment to appreciate the valuable lessons learned and opportunities presented by the gift that is your hangover. For example:

- It's now a great excuse to indulge in comfort foods
- You can bond with friends over shared stories from the night before
- It's a chance to catch up on the Netflix series you've been meaning to watch
- Your body has staged a protest. If it's a particularly loud and disorderly protest, bear this in mind for next time

# 5.
# LOSING CONTROL

Lie on the floor and see if you can change TV channels – or control your preferred device – using only your toes. Once you've mastered that, try it with your nose and any other body part that tickles your fancy

# **LORD OF THE HANGOVERS**

Come up with five films where a word in the title can be replaced by "hangover". Here's some to get you going:

1. The Hangover Games *(The Hunger Games)*
2. The Lord of the Hangover *(The Lord of the Rings)*
3. Harry Potter and the Deathly Hangover *(Harry Potter and the Deathly Hallows)*
4. Pirates of the Caribbean: At World's Hangover *(Pirates of the Caribbean: At World's End)*
5. Indiana Jones and the Last Hangover *(Indiana Jones and the Last Crusade)*

# 7.

## LAUGH AWAY THE PAIN

Place a small piece of tape over the bottom of someone's computer mouse. Watch as your victim tries to figure out why their pointing device isn't working. Bonus points for drawing a smiley face on the tape

# DETOX YOGA POSES

Feel better as you try out these yoga moves
(which double up as convenient nap positions)

# 9.

# WOULD YOU RATHER?

1. Would you rather spend the day, badly hungover, trying to solve a Rubik's Cube or attempting to assemble a piece of IKEA furniture with missing parts?

2. Would you rather wake up after a night of drinking and find a tattoo of a cartoon character on your arm or discover that you've accidentally shaved off one eyebrow?

3. Would you rather have to endure a day of non-stop hiccups or have every food you eat taste like soggy cardboard for the entire day?

# 10.

## HISTORICAL HANGOVERS

**Want to know what the cure was for hangovers before aspirin was invented?**

The Roman philosopher Pliny the Elder recommended eating raw owl's eggs or fried canary. By the Middle Ages, a go-to remedy was to gulp down some raw eel and bitter almonds

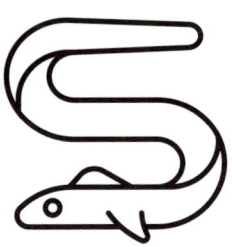

# 11.

# ALTERNATIVE HANGOVER RECOVERY IDEAS

According to Puerto Ricans, rubbing a slice of lemon under your armpits before a heavy drinking session will ease the headache later on – worth a go for next time?

A traditional Polish hangover cure is to drink pickle juice the morning after a heavy night

Some people swear by tomato juice and raw eggs. That might sound disgusting, but the egg yolk contains amino acids and the tomato juice is rich in antioxidants and vitamins

# 12.

## OOPS, I DID IT AGAIN

Draft a heartfelt apology to your neighbours for your regrettable antics last night. Especially the one whose plant pot you peed in

*I'm Sorry*

# 13.

## DIY HANGOVER KIT

Create your own hangover survival kit with items like painkillers, electrolyte drinks and healthy snacks. Bonus points for creative packaging!

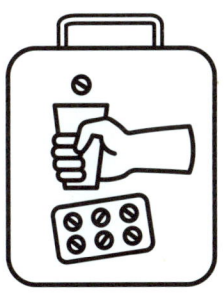

# 14.

## MOCKTAIL MIXOLOGIST

Create a hangover-friendly mocktail with unexpected ingredients found in your fridge. Make it taste so good that it will make you forget alcohol ever existed

# 15.

## FEEL LIKE THE WORLD IS JUST TOO NOISY RIGHT NOW?

Consider this instead: as well as being the world's biggest animal, the blue whale is also one of the loudest. Its calls can reach up to 188 decibels, which is louder than a jet engine and can be heard from hundreds of miles away

# 16.

## NETFLIX ROULETTE

Close your eyes and pick a random movie or TV show on Netflix and watch it without reading the description or viewing the trailer. It's time to embrace the element of surprise

## 17.

### EASE YOUR GUILT WITH THIS WISE QUOTE...

# "ALCOHOL MAY NOT SOLVE YOUR PROBLEMS, BUT NEITHER WILL MILK."

*Anonymous*

# 18.

## NOSTALGIA BINGE

Crack out old books, toys or games that you remember fondly from childhood – or get online and find photos and video clips of these comforting cultural creations. Hopefully the sweet kiss of nostalgia will take the edge off that splitting headache

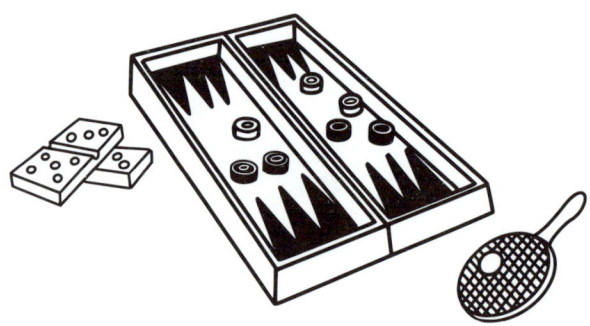

# 19.

## HANGOVER HAIRSTYLES

Experiment with outrageous new hairstyles to distract from your hangover-induced malaise. Document your creations with selfies and share the pics online (or maybe just with trusted friends)

## 20.
## SOFA SHAPE-UP

Right now, start a five-day fitness challenge that you can complete without even leaving your sofa. How about kicking off with the Cushion Crunch, the TV Twist and the Sofa Squat, followed of course by the Lazy Leg Lift

## 21.

## READ A BOOK

Pick up that book you've been meaning to start for ages and blow off the dust. Today is a brand-new day. Here are some famous books which explore hangovers and which you might like to try (the books, not the hangovers):

**The Sun Also Rises**
by Ernest Hemingway

**Bright Lights, Big City**
by Jay McInerney

**Fear and Loathing in Las Vegas**
by Hunter S. Thompson

## 22.
### BUTTER UP

> Pay someone a heartfelt compliment, then very quickly ask if they can make you a sandwich

## 23.

## BECOME A WATER SNOB

Transform yourself into a water connoisseur and taste-test five different bottled waters, noting the subtle differences. Which brand is your favourite and why?

If you're feeling creative, write a short review in the style of a snooty critic

_____

_____

_____

_____

_____

_____

## 24.
# BLOW YOUR MIND WITH THESE FOODIE FACTS

**Bananas are berries, but strawberries aren't**

**Peanuts aren't nuts; they're legumes**

**Apples float in water because around 25% of their volume is air**

**The word "avocado" comes from the Aztec word "ahuacatl", which means "testicle"**

## 25.
# FROZEN SURPRISE

Freeze one of your friend's belongings, like their house keys, in a block of ice and then reveal your handiwork to your victim – just make sure they will see the funny side (eventually) and you don't destroy a priceless object

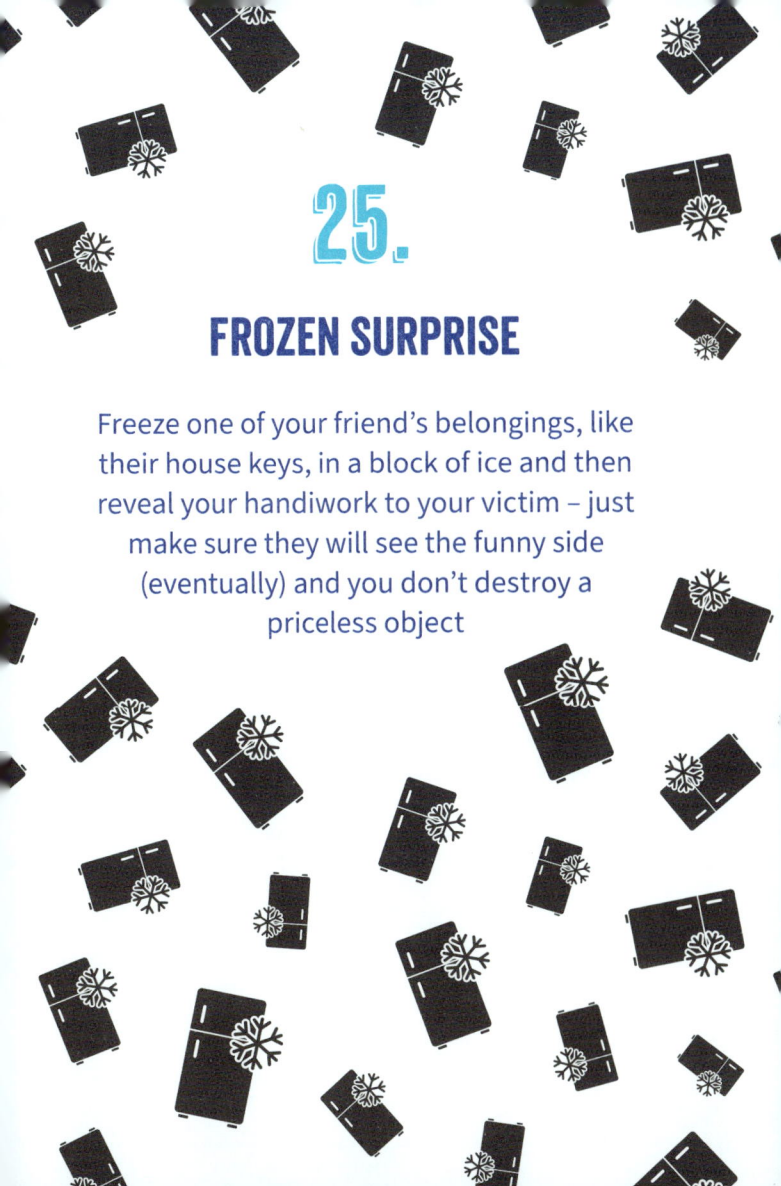

# 26.

## SET OFF A SMILE AVALANCHE

Go for a walk around the block and smile at five different people (in the least creepy way possible, please) and see if they smile back

# 27.

## HANGOVER ANTHEM PLAYLIST

Compile a playlist of songs that perfectly encapsulates the hangover experience. How about "Hair of the Dog" by Nazareth, "Hungover" by Kesha, or "Sunday Morning Coming Down" by Johnny Cash?

# 28.

## WRITE A BALLAD

If you're now in a musical mood, grab your preferred instrument and compose your own hangover ballad or boozy banger. If you're tone deaf and lack the equipment, just bash out an extended drum solo on your bed or sofa. Rock and roll

# 29.

## PONDER THIS INSTEAD OF YOUR HANGOVER

In the 1920s, the world's population was approximately 2 billion humans. It has now surpassed 8 billion, quadrupling in less than a century and still rising all the time – that's more and more hangovers every single day

# 30.

## LITTLE JOYS

List the five things you love doing most. Write them down and make a pact with yourself to do them more regularly

# 31.

## HANGOVER HIDE-AND-SEEK

Set up a game of hide-and-seek in your house, but with a twist. Whoever's seeking has to do it blindfolded while the hiders quietly make hangover-related noises

## 32.

## PRACTISE THE "I'M FINE" FAÇADE

Perfect your post-hangover poker face in the mirror, then hold an imaginary conversation with someone who thinks you had a very heavy night last night. Deny the charges like a very shady politician

# 33.

## iHANGOVER

**What if your hangover could give a TED Talk?**

Consider what topics would it cover and whether anyone would actually attend. OK, now go watch a proper TED Talk to see how it's done

# 34.

## HANGOVER HYPOTHETICALS

Quiz your friends with these outrageous hypothetical scenarios:

- Would it be better to have your boss show up unannounced while you're still in your pyjamas or have your ex call you during your worst hangover ever?

- Would it be better to wake up with a piercing in a random body part or wake up with a stranger's phone number tattooed on your arm?

- Would it be better to have your entire night out documented and posted on social media or wake up in a completely different city with no memory of how you got there?

# 35.

## MEMORY MATCH

Test your friends' memories by seeing who can recall the most embarrassing moments from the night before. The person with the most detailed recollection is the winner (or maybe the loser)!

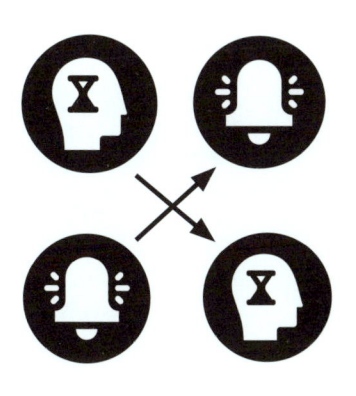

## 36.

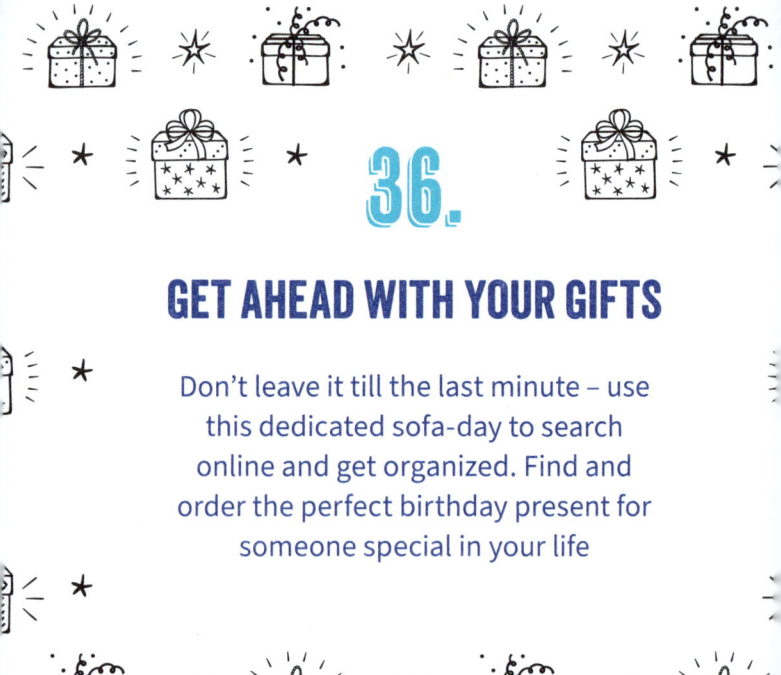

## GET AHEAD WITH YOUR GIFTS

Don't leave it till the last minute – use this dedicated sofa-day to search online and get organized. Find and order the perfect birthday present for someone special in your life

# 37.

# PLAY BLANKET BURRITOS WITH YOUR FRIENDS

## LEVEL 1: THE COSY ROLL

Roll yourself up in a blanket like a burrito and see who can roll the tightest without falling

## LEVEL 2: BURRITO BOWLING

Set up a bowling alley in the living room using empty water bottles as pins and take turns rolling yourself like a burrito to knock them down

## LEVEL 3: THE BURRITO BALANCE

See how long you can balance like a burrito on one foot while wrapped up in a blanket

# 38.

## INVENT A NEW DANCE MOVE

Your body might feel like it's being inhabited by grumpy wasps right now, but put on some music and get it moving to dance away the pain. Come up with a new move and give it a suitable name – The Reanimated Corpse, perhaps

## 39.

## HUNGOVER CHARADES

Play a game of charades where all the clues are related to the hangover experiences or items associated with a night of drinking. Players have to act out phrases like "pounding headache" or "greasy food craving" while their teammates guess

## 40.

## REMEMBER, THIS TOO SHALL PASS...

Hangover symptoms typically peak around mid-morning, roughly 8 to 12 hours after your last drink, when your blood-alcohol concentration returns to zero but he symptoms rarely last more than 24 hours.

So, if you're feeling really rough after a heavy night out, it will only get better…

# 41.
# PODCAST POSSIBILITIES

Outline to a friend a podcast series you'd host, complete with three episode titles and three guest ideas, and see what they think.

Try roleplaying the first interview and recording it for a laugh

## 42.

## CONVINCE YOUR PET THAT YOU'RE NOT DYING

You might even get a free, comforting cuddle – just remember to keep your furry friend fed and well hydrated in solidarity

# 43.

## OUT WITH THE OLD

Go to your wardrobe and pick out five things you don't really need, then donate them to charity. While you're at the charity shop, you might even find a treasure.

In 1989, a man browsing through a flea market in Pennsylvania stumbled upon a painting that had hidden behind it an original printed copy of the Declaration of Independence. The print, known as a **"Dunlap Broadside"**, was one of only 24 surviving copies from 1776.

**It was later sold at auction for $2.42 million**

## 44.

## FANTASY FORTUNE

If you won an enormous amount of money, decide how you would spend it. Would you give any away? It could happen.

In 2016, three ticket holders in the United States shared the Powerball prize of $1.586 billion. And in November 2022, one lucky Californian won the biggest-ever jackpot of $2.04 billion.

# 45.

## YEAR-IN-A-BOX

Which five things would you choose to put in a time capsule to represent this year so far (and to confuse future archaeologists)?

1. ........................................................
2. ........................................................
3. ........................................................
4. ........................................................
5. ........................................................

## 46.

## TOGA PARADE

Wrap yourself in your bedsheet and take a solemn walk of honour to the nearest coffee shop, ordering your drink with the name "Caesar"

# 47.

## GLOBETROTTER

Choose ten places you want to visit in the next ten years and then see if you can point out where they are on a blank map of the world (you can find these online)

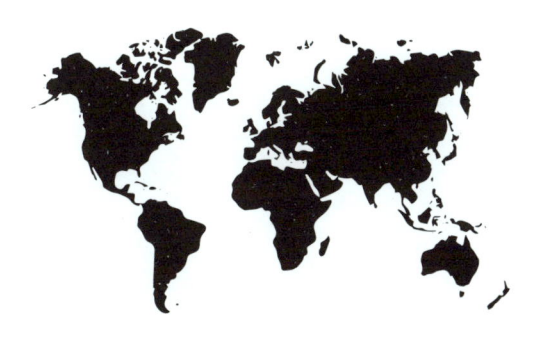

## 48.

## HANGOVER OLYMPICS

Organize a hangover-friendly Olympic Games with your friends.

Events might include:

- The Pillow Plunge
- The Nap-Off
- The Hangover Hurdles
- The Longest Burp
- The Movie Marathon

## 49.
### STEAL THIS LEGENDARY LINE

## "I feel sorry for people who don't drink. When they wake up in the morning, that's as good as they're going to feel all day."

It's not certain who coined this quip – it's been attributed variously to Jack Lemmon, W.C. Fields, Frank Sinatra and Dean Martin – so maybe try to pass it off as your own wit and wisdom next time you're out on the town

# 50.

## FAREWELL FEASTS

If you only had five more meals before this hangover killed you, decide what they would be

## 51.

# THERE WAS A BEST BUD...

Write a hilarious limerick about your best pal and then text it to them. Here are some words that rhyme with "drunk" to get you started:

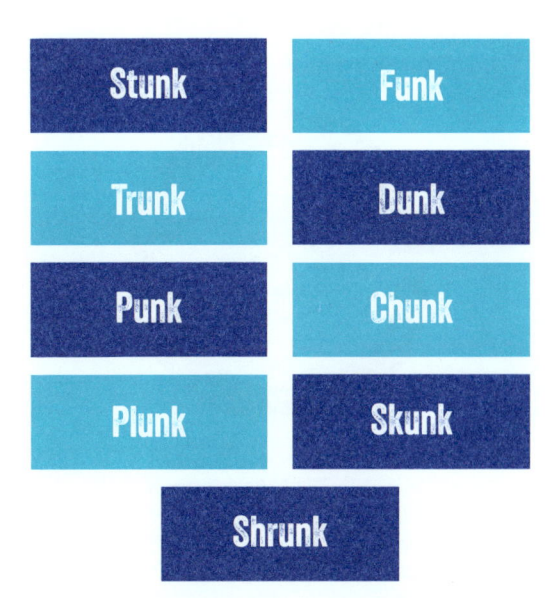

| Stunk | Funk |
| --- | --- |
| Trunk | Dunk |
| Punk | Chunk |
| Plunk | Skunk |

Shrunk

## 52.
# SWITCHEROO

Swap the contents of food or drink containers in the fridge, then watch your hungry hungover friends or loved ones have a total brain meltdown

# 53.

## HANGOVER HOBBY HOUR

Dedicate an hour to trying out a new hobby that you've always been curious about but never had the time to pursue. How about calligraphy, photography, journaling or painting? Embrace the soothing distraction from your hangover woes

## 54.

# WATERMELON WHIRLWIND

Slice up a juicy watermelon with your friends and see who can devour their piece the fastest, hands-free. Bonus points for creativity and style

# 55.

# THE HANGOVER CHRONICLES

Watch and rate these movies with classic hangover scenes:

- Dude, Where's My Car? (2000)
- Withnail and I (1987)
- Bridesmaids (2011)
- Arthur (1981)
- The Hangover (2009)
- Leaving Las Vegas (1995)

# 56.
## THE REVERSE ROOM

Rearrange your hungover friend's bedroom in a mirror image of how it usually is. Swap the position of the bed, move the dresser to the opposite side of the room, and so on. When they wake up groggy and disoriented, they'll be greeted with a room that looks oddly familiar yet completely different

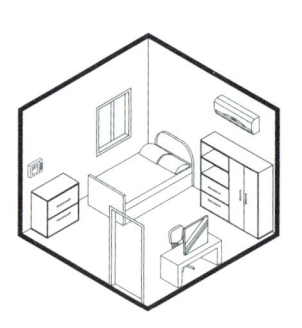

# 57.

## SOLVE THIS "WHAT AM I?" PUZZLE...

I'm often found in bottles,
but I'm not a genie.
Pour me in a glass,
and your night will get dreamy.
Some call me "firewater",
some call me "booze",
After a few too many,
you might sing the blues.
What am I?

(Answer: alcohol, obviously)

# 58.

## THE PILLOW PINNACLE

See how tall a tower you can build with pillows and cushions found in your living room. Then send a pic to a friend and challenge them to beat your mighty edifice

# 59.
## READ YOUR HANGOVER HOROSCOPE

| ARIES | Your hangover is a battle scar |
|---|---|
| TAURUS | Take it slow and steady today |
| GEMINI | Embrace your hangover with wit and a Bloody Mary |
| CANCER | Seek refuge in the comfort of your home |
| LEO | Pamper yourself like royalty |
| VIRGO | Nourish your body with wholesome foods |
| LIBRA | Surround yourself with loved ones |
| SCORPIO | Embrace the transformative power of your hangover through creativity |
| SAGITTARIUS | Embrace chaos and explore new experiences with optimism |
| CAPRICORN | Take a break from responsibilities |
| AQUARIUS | Embrace your eccentricity and find humour in the situation |
| PISCES | Take refuge in your imagination and heal through dreams |

# 60.

## SOLVE THIS PROBLEM

You're planning a wine-tasting event and have three different types of wine: red, white and rosé.

You want to provide each guest with a tasting flight consisting of one glass of each type of wine. If each bottle contains 750 ml of wine and a standard wine glass holds 150 ml, how many guests can you invite with your available wine if you have five bottles of each type of wine?

*(Answer: 25)*

# 61.

## LAST NIGHT LIVE

Write down in a notebook some funny observations about last night that you'd include in your debut stand-up routine and thereby turn messy embarrassment into comedy gold

## 62.

# HISTORICAL HIJINKS

Grab a notebook and write a three-line pitch for a historical time-travel adventure.

**Which eras would be visited and just how messed up would the future get by characters interfering in the past?**

_____

_____

_____

# 63.

# LEARN SOMETHING NEW RIGHT NOW

Here are three words, and their meanings, which you may not know:

**Bibulous**
fond of alcoholic beverages

**Crepuscular**
relating to twilight

**Callipygian**
having shapely buttocks

## 64.

# THE GREAT BREAKFAST DEBATE

Decide on your top five must-haves out of these choices:

**CHOOSE YOUR TOP FIVE MUST-HAVES**

1. Bacon
2. Sausages
3. Eggs
4. Baked beans
5. Grilled tomatoes
6. Hash browns
7. Mushrooms
8. Toast

# 65.

## IT COULD BE WORSE

Think of the ten things you would least like to do today. Get creative with it and then write a one-page piece of flash fiction based on one of your horrifying options

## 66.

# THE SOUND OF WAILING AND GNASHING OF TEETH

List the five songs you would least like to listen to with a hangover – then send links to the music videos of these terrible tunes to your hungover friends, recommending the music as a cure for all their ills

1. ..................................................................
2. ..................................................................
3. ..................................................................
4. ..................................................................
5. ..................................................................

## 67.

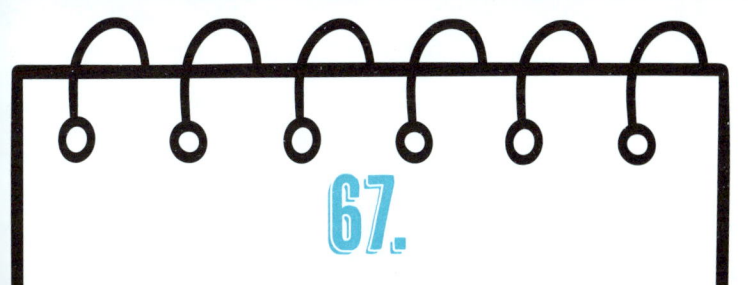

# EXTREME HANGOVER DEN

Plan a room renovation in your house with an unlimited budget. Here's some ideas to get you started:

- ✓ A retractable roof
- ✓ A built-in espresso bar
- ✓ A transparent wall revealing an aquarium
- ✓ A stage in your dining room
- ✓ Floor-to-ceiling bookshelves
- ✓ A glass-roofed oasis filled with exotic plants
- ✓ Floor-to-ceiling screens that wrap around the entire room

## 68.

## LEARN ABOUT DRUNKEN CELEBRITIES

During the Second World War, **Winston Churchill** was known for his love of whisky and champagne. He was said to have a daily routine that included starting the day with a whisky and soda and continuing with wine and brandy thereafter. Despite his heavy drinking, he led Britain through some of its darkest hours with wit and resolve.

**André the Giant**, a French professional wrestler and actor, who was dubbed "the Eighth Wonder of the World", would drink beer as a warm-up before a wrestling match and reportedly could get through more than 100 beers in one night.

# 69.

# HAVE A BREAKFAST BUFFET BED PICNIC

Why go out for brunch when you can have a smorgasbord of snacks while wrapped in the comfort of your duvet? And instead of a traditional fry up, consider one of these traditional breakfasts instead:

**Japan's natto**
*fermented soybeans*

**Colombia's changua**
*milk soup with eggs poached in it*

**Iceland's hákarl**
*fermented shark meat*

**Ethiopia's injera**
*a spongy, sour flatbread*

# 70.

## PLAY SLOW-MOTION TAG

It is exactly like regular tag, but at a pace that won't make your head spin or induce vomiting

## 71.

## GIVE YOUR FUTURE SELF A GIFT

Let's face it: this day is a write-off. Embrace the grimness of it and make your future self much happier by doing that one tiresome chore or tricky job you've been putting off for ages.

# "THANKS, HUNGOVER ME," YOU'LL SAY. "I OWE YOU A DRINK!"

# 72.

## SIGNATURE SWAGGER

Practise your autograph. You never know when you might need it.

**Did you know that the world's most sought-after autograph is from… a doctor?** Doctors' signatures are so valuable because they're the only ones that can get you out of work – with a legitimate excuse!

## 73.

# THE FIVE STAGES OF HANGOVER GRIEF

Decide where you are right now in the hangover experience:

**DENIAL**

**ANGER**

**BARGAINING**

**DEPRESSION**

**ACCEPTANCE**

# 74.

## DOUGH DRIVE

Call a bakery and ask if you can borrow some dough to buy a new car. If it's a no, ask them if they have any dad jokes like that one

## 75.

## MEMORY MASH

Try to remember what Thing 72 was without peeking. Pass or fail, now try memorizing pi to as many decimal places as you can manage. Here it is with 20 of them for starters:

**3.14159265358979323846**


## 76.

## RECOVERY HOTLINE

Set up a group chat where friends can share their hangover woes and offer support. Bonus points for creative hangover-themed emojis

# 77.

## ZOMBIE WALK

Stumble around a local footpath or hiking trail groaning like a zombie.

When fellow walkers look concerned, just tell them you're practising for an upcoming role in *The Walking Dead: The Morning After*

# 78.

## HANGOVER HANGMAN

Play a game of hangman with hangover-themed words or phrases. See who can guess the phrase with the fewest incorrect guesses and come up with hilarious penalties for losers. Here are some suggestions:

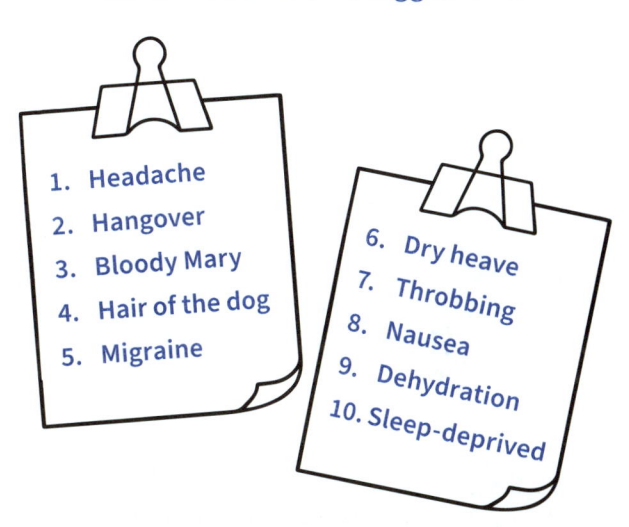

1. Headache
2. Hangover
3. Bloody Mary
4. Hair of the dog
5. Migraine
6. Dry heave
7. Throbbing
8. Nausea
9. Dehydration
10. Sleep-deprived

# 79.

## MATCH THE NATIONAL ANIMALS WITH THEIR COUNTRIES

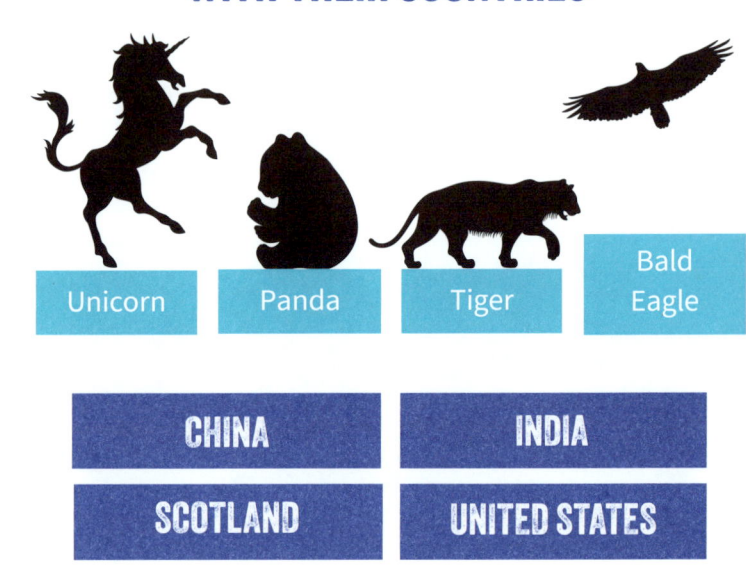

Unicorn  Panda  Tiger  Bald Eagle

CHINA

INDIA

SCOTLAND

UNITED STATES

*( Answer: China: Panda, India: Tiger, Scotland: Unicorn, United States: Bald Eagle )*

# 80.

# HANGOVER HYDROTHERAPY

Transform your bathroom into a makeshift spa by filling the tub with ice-cold water and adding a few refreshing citrus slices. Then, take turns plunging into the chilly depths to shock your system awake and rejuvenate your senses

# 81.

## ULTIMATE ROAD TRIP PLAYLIST

Curate the perfect road trip playlist from "setting out" to "are we there yet?" Then decide where you're going to go

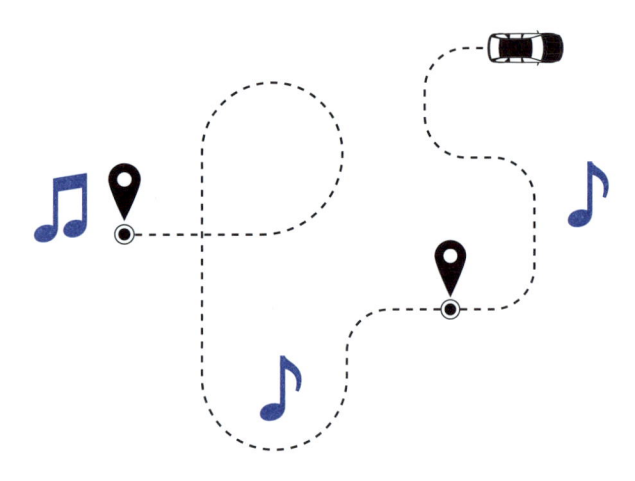

## 82.

# BREWERY BUCKET LIST

Plan a tour of the top five breweries
you would most like to visit

**How about one of the most famous breweries in the world?**
Established in 1759 in Dublin, the Guinness Brewery at St James's Gate is known for its iconic stout beer

**Or you could go to the Dogfish Head Brewery, based in Delaware, USA.**
Known for its innovative approach to brewing, the company even recreates beer recipes from archaeological discoveries

## 83.

# HANGOVER HANGUL LESSON

Learn the Korean alphabet, Hangul, and teach your hungover friends how to read and write simple phrases. It's a fun way to pass the time while nursing your hangover – and it might come in handy for future travels

GOOD NIGHT!
잘자!

# 84.

## CULINARY WORLD TOUR

Plan a three-course fusion meal with ingredients and inspiration from three different corners of the globe, and then – if you have the energy, the money and the skills – set about making it and sharing it with your favourite person (or just take the lazy option and order in some comfort food for yourself)

# 85.

## STAR DOUBLE

Consider which actor would be perfectly cast to play you in a movie about your life. What would be the title for the film?

## 86.

## HACK ATTACK

What's your best life hack that the world (or just your friendship group) needs to know? Here's one for nothing:

> Put your phone in a bowl or cup to amplify its sound. It's like having your own portable speaker system, minus the hassle of wires or Bluetooth connections

## 87.

## ME MUSEUM

**Which four or five items would be in a museum exhibit about you?**
Collect them up and make a mini display – then take a pic for posterity

> **CONGRATS!**
> You've turned a potentially wasted day into a worthy cultural exercise

## 88.
## HAVE A LAUGH

**Q:** Why don't skeletons fight each other?

**A:** They don't have the guts!

.................................................

**Q:** Why don't scientists trust atoms?

**A:** Because they make up everything!

.................................................

**Q:** Why did the scarecrow win an award?

**A:** Because he was outstanding in his field!

# 89.
## REMEMBER, YOU ARE NOT ALONE

Almost every person alive today has tiny bugs, called *Demodex* mites, living inside the pores of their face, especially in and around the eyelashes. Most of the time these little eyelash mites won't bother you, and you won't even know they're there, but take comfort in the fact that you're not going through this hangover alone

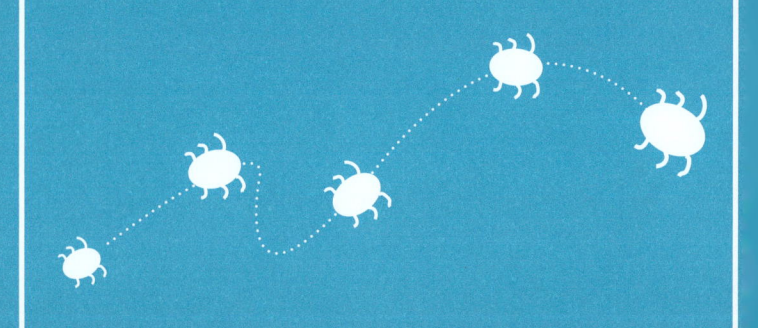

# 90.

# CEREAL BOX PUZZLE

Flatten a cereal box and cut it into pieces. Mix them up and put the "puzzle" back together. Well done, champ

## 91.

## SUPER SELF

**Create a superhero version of yourself – what's your special power?**

**Sketch your costume on some paper, and be sure to include your cape and any signature weapons**

# 92.
# FILL YOUR BRAIN WITH RANDOM NATURE FACTS

Butterflies taste with their feet

Bees dance to communicate with each other

Sea otters hold hands while sleeping to keep from drifting apart

## 93.

## WAKE-UP CALL

If anyone in your house is sleeping, wake them up and tell them a weird-looking 7-foot man is at the door and he urgently needs to speak to them

# 94.
# CREATE A ROYAL MIX-UP

Call McDonald's and ask them for the phone number of Burger King

# 95.

## THE HANGOVER FAIRY TALE

Find a notebook (or the notes app on your phone) and write a short story beginning with the opening line:

**Once Upon a Regrettable Night...**

## 96.

# KITCHEN CHALLENGE

Try fixing yourself a yummy treat using only one hand, just to keep things interesting. Here are some ideas to get you started:

**BANANAS:** Rich in potassium, bananas can help replenish electrolytes

**TOAST:** This can help settle your stomach

**AVOCADO:** Packed with healthy fats and potassium, avocados can support liver function

**EGGS:** They're a good source of protein and contain cysteine, which can help break down acetaldehyde, a toxic by-product of alcohol metabolism

**YOGURT:** This is easy on the stomach and contains probiotics

**GINGER TEA:** It's long been used to soothe upset stomachs

# 97.

## HANGOVER HAUTE COUTURE

Change into your ultimate hangover outfit. Does it include indoor sunglasses and a statement coffee mug?

## 98.
## SORT YOUR LIFE OUT

### DECLUTTER YOUR DESK
Organize your workspace by getting rid of unnecessary papers and items

### DIGITAL DETOX
Take a break from social media by temporarily deactivating your accounts or limiting your screen time

### UNSUBSCRIBE SPREE
Unsubscribe from newsletters and promotional emails that clutter your inbox

### PHOTO & APP PURGE
Go through your digital photo library and delete duplicates or photos you no longer need. Delete unused apps from your phone or computer to free up storage space

## 99.

## HANGOVER HALL OF SHAME

Who are the four celebrities you would least like to spend a hangover day with?
How about:

- CHARLIE SHEEN
- LINDSAY LOHAN
- JUSTIN BIEBER
- KANYE WEST

Now be grateful it's just you and your headache

# 100.

## CONSIDER WHY BEER IS LIKE FOOTBALL...

| | |
|---|---|
| **Ups and Downs:** Highs and lows are expected during a football match, and beer-drinking can also bring you moments of joy and misery | **Community:** Both beer festivals and football matches serve as opportunities for communities to come together and celebrate shared interests |
| **Tradition:** Beer and football often come with their own set of traditions, from pre-game gatherings to post-match celebrations | **Passion:** Just as football fans are known for their dedication to their teams, beer enthusiasts can be equally crazy about their favourite brews |

# 101.

## SWEAR OFF SPIRITS, FOR NOW

Write a note to your future self, describing just how bad this hangover is. Include all the gory details so you'll be warned to never drink again (until next time)